To Annette & Howard

On your new home,
its wonderful & special!

Love, Kathy & Ben

Aug, 1993

HOUSE
WARMINGS

*For those who make
a house a home*

HOUSE
WARMINGS

*For those who make
a house a home*

by Patricia Houck Sprinkle
Illustrated by Gail Roth

The C.R. Gibson Company, Norwalk, Connecticut 06856

❖

Dedicated to Mother, Dad,
and Priscilla,
and the homes we shared.

❖

*We shape our buildings and afterwards
our buildings shape us.*
Winston Churchill

❖

Foreword

Growing up as the daughter of a minister and then becoming a minister's wife, I have lived in over twenty houses in my life. Sometimes the chaos of moving threatens to overwhelm me. As I wend my way around boxes, stacks of unshelved books, mountains of dishes, I am tempted to sit down and resign from living.

That's when I try to remember that in the beginning the whole universe was chaos—a swirling, formless mass. Then came light, order, and life.

So, to create a home is a very God-like thing: we breathe into that space our personal spirit and make it in our own image.

I have also discovered that homes provide lessons for living. These I share in the hope that they will inspire you as you make your house a home.

Patricia H. Sprinkle

> *The house of everyone is . . . castle and fortress,*
> *as well for defense against injury*
> *and violence as for repose.*
>
> Sir Edward Coke

When I was five years old, my friend Libby and I built string houses.

Taking a fat ball of white cotton string, we tied it waist-high around the sycamore near her porch. Then we wound it around each tree in her yard until we had a huge rough circle. To make rooms, we tied pieces of string across the center.

We always put the living room in the front and the kitchen in the back. The bathroom—a smuggled roll of toilet paper—was under the big snowball bush, and the bedroom was that space between the living room and the kitchen.

We would play house for hours. Finally, exhausted, we would declare "night." With a blanket and two pillows from her bed, we would lie down to take a long nap.

As an adult, I marvel at how we trusted those string walls.

We would never have simply lain on the grass to sleep. We were too afraid of stray dogs, cats, and neighborhood boys. Yet inside the walls of our "house"—one piece of white string tied two feet from the ground—we slept absolutely secure.

Since the dawn of time people have built houses. Some are no more than walls of woven straw or canvas. Some are a layer of brick, insulation, four-inch studs, and drywall. They protect us from prying eyes, cold, and rain. They give boundaries to what is "ours." Within them, most of us feel secure.

Yet, if we are wise, we have to admit that our security does not come from strong walls. Few of them would withstand determined assault. Security comes instead from what we build inside those walls:

- a haven of peace and beauty in an often chaotic world;

- a web of relationships that holds firm through outside storms;

- a place where we can safely store family skeletons and take off our masks;

- a temple of faith in Someone with power to truly protect.

Let us build well inside our walls. Then, whether our walls are stone or string, we can sleep secure.

You may have to live in a crowd,
but you do not have to live like it,
nor subsist on its food.
You may have your own orchard.
You may drink at a hidden spring.
Be yourself if you would serve others.
Henry Van Dyke

F riends have just moved into their new home. They have one dining table and a year-old daughter. Will they buy a second dining table for the breakfast room, or turn that space into a playroom for their child?

Our own first apartment had three rooms: a kitchen, a living/dining room, and a bedroom. Bob was finishing graduate school, I worked and did free-lance writing in the evenings. And we were constantly in one another's way.

He tried studying on the dining table, but had to move for every meal. I tried writing in bed, but kept falling asleep amid manuscript sheets. Finally one evening we sat down and looked at our lives. We seldom entertained, and ate one meal a day in the apartment. Why, then, devote one whole room to what we seldom did, when we needed work space more?

We decided to sleep and eat in the same room and buy desks for the larger room. What a relief to exchange boxed notions of what rooms we "should" have for the spaces we really needed!

The world likes to dictate how we use our space—and how we use our lives. Builders name certain rooms and expect us to shape our lives to fit them. It takes creativity to designate rooms for unusual uses that suit our own needs.

We know a single man who eats in his living room because his pool table fills his "dining" room. We have friends who filled their "formal living room" with computer equipment and use their "den" for all living room functions.

Similarly, society has boxed expectations for who we should be and what we should do. It takes courage to build a unique marriage, raise unique children, become a unique person.

We would know mankind better
if we were not so anxious to resemble one another.
Goethe

Be ever soft and pliable like a reed,
not hard and unbending like a cedar.
The Talmud

I want a house that has got over all its troubles;
I don't want to spend the rest of my life
bringing up a young and inexperienced house.

Jerome K. Jerome

The first house we bought was built in 1900. It was large, with gracious rooms. It was also cheap, because it was condemned.

Equipped with youth, two incomes, and lots of energy, we spent all our leisure time and most of our money on that house. When other new homeowners groan about having to rip out walls, tear off a roof, sand floors, scrub and paint walls, install wiring or plumbing, we know exactly what they mean!

We cried over errors, battled over color schemes, and ached from our labors. Sometimes I felt the house itself weep and ache.

As we worked on that house, however, we discovered to our surprise we were also working on ourselves!

As we sanded rough floors and woodwork, we sanded off the rough edges of our marriage;

as we scrubbbed ceilings and walls, we cleaned up bad tempers and lazy habits;

as we learned to install new plumbing, drywall, and a bathroom floor, we developed the habit of learning new skills;

as we dreamed about what the house could become, we dared to dream about what we ourselves might become.

If we pay attention to the lessons, working on a house can teach patience, cooperation, perseverance, and hope. We can learn that worthwhile things can take a long time, but are worth working and even fighting for. We can learn to look beneath roughness or grime for possibilities—in people, as well as in houses.

And we can learn that when relationships, experiences, and disappointments rub and scrub us painfully, they may just be helping us realize our full potential!

Old houses, I thought,
do not belong to people ever, not really,
people belong to them.

Gladys Taylor

He who has come through the fire
will not fade in the sun.

Hindu Proverb

Rejoice with those who rejoice,
weep with those who weep.
Saint Paul

There is something about working on houses that quickly brings fellow sufferers together. You stop on sidewalks to ask the fastest way to take off paint. You pause in the grocery store to discuss cheap places to rent floor sanders, and groan together about the housing inspector's most recent visit. And have you noticed how helpful people are to one another in home builders' supply stores?

Whenever you despair of making progress on your own project, it helps to stroll around to another house in worse shape. And after a hard Saturday of scrubbing walls, what joy to collapse and laugh with others who also ache in every joint!

Sometimes we think it is virtuous to be self sufficient. When we suffer, we think it best to suffer alone. Working on a house, however, shows us how suffering can be eased by sharing it with others who truly understand, how to put our own sufferings into perspective by considering others who suffer more—even how to laugh in our pain! Those lessons are not just about home repair sufferings. They work for life's sorrows and struggles, as well.

Work without joy shall be as nothing.
Resolve to be happy, and your joy and you shall form
an invincible host against difficulties.
Helen Keller

What was hard to bear is sweet to remember.

Portuguese Proverb

I t took us a year to get hot water piped to our "temporary" attic kitchen. Until we did, we carried dishpans from the bathroom, through the bedroom, and across the kitchen. Then we washed dishes under a sloped roof that forced us to lean to one side. It took almost that long to get a bathroom floor upstairs. Until then we walked along the rafters, hoping we wouldn't fall off and crash through the dining room ceiling.

To this day I am grateful every time I turn on a kitchen faucet and get hot water, can stand erect at a dishpan, or cross a tiled bathroom floor!

What other blessings do we take for granted, when doing without them for a time would make it clear how precious they are?

hen we moved to Florida, we had no idea what kind of house to look for. After three years restoring the old house, we thought almost any house would do so long as it didn't need years of work. We planned to choose one in a morning.

The first house we looked at had upper cupboards too high for me to reach without a stool. The only bath was upstairs, which meant our friend in a wheelchair couldn't visit. "But," Bob said wistfully, "I'd like being this near the water."

The next house reeked with the odor of four German shepherd dogs. Choking, we sought refuge in the back yard—and were charmed by a glossy full-grown orange tree just coming into fruit.

The next house was on a corner with traffic whizzing by. How could we hope to have and raise children there? "But," I noticed, "a corner house does get a lot of light. I like that."

And so it went. One house had no place for me to write, but it did have a wonderful living room for meetings. Another's tiny living/dining room would never let us entertain as we like to, but we liked its Spanish stucco style.

After two days we were exhausted, despairing, and bewildered. What was the matter with us? We'd already lived in a condemned place. Why were we so picky now?

"All we need, Lord," Bob prayed lightly, "is a Spanish-style stucco house with a big living room and dining room, a place for Patti to write, low cabinets, and orange trees."

"On a quiet corner near the water," I added with a laugh.

Guess what we found the very next day? For the next five years we lived in a stucco house on a quiet corner one block from Tampa Bay. I wrote in a small, peaceful study. We entertained friends in our large living and dining rooms. Our first son played under our orange tree. I cooked in a kitchen custom-built for a woman even shorter than I! That house was precisely what we needed to relax after work, entertain friends, raise our first child, and grow toward the people we are becoming.

Where did we ever get the notion that it is "selfish" to seek homes, jobs, partners, and ways of living that best suit who we are? When will we discover that each of us has been created unique, and blossoms best in certain soils? When will we learn to ask for what we need—and give other people freedom to ask for what they need, too?

If you do not express your own original ideas,
if you do not listen to your own being,
then you will have betrayed yourself.

Rollo May

*I would dedicate this nation
to the policy of the good neighbor.*
Franklin Delano Roosevelt

I will never forget that moving day in Chicago. To be near our work, we bought within the city limits on a block where we would be the only white family. As we unloaded our truck, the family across the street sat on their porch and shouted, "Honky, go home!" Five years later, just before we moved away, I sat on that same front porch drinking iced tea and talking lazily with my neighbor. "I'm gonna miss you," she said.

"I'm gonna miss you, too," I agreed.

What made the difference?

We had worked together in a neighborhood block club, trying to build a safer community in which to live.

We had laughed together when I planted five forsythia bushes and two of them came up lilacs.

We had grieved together when she discovered her grandson had a speech impediment, and when my son broke a leg.

We were lazy together, drinking tea on her porch or my front steps when it was too hot to do anything else.

We didn't have much in common. Gulfs of temperament and interests were far greater than our different skin colors. But as I stood to leave, she summed it up in one sentence. "You've kinda grown on me. While you've been here, we've been good neighbors."

Since those early, stormy days in Chicago, I have tried to be a better neighbor.

uilding a house is a humbling experience. It's easy, living in a home built by others, to grumble at its imperfections and wonder why the people who built it couldn't have done a better job. When it is our own house, however, when we've made all the calculations and designs, when we have spent hours bullying the builder, why does the pantry door swing out too far? Why is the bathroom counter not long enough? Why does the fireplace smoke? If we are honest, we have to admit it is because we are not perfect people.

We have two choices at that point: we can fume and fret at our own inadequacies, or we can learn to accept our own limitations and, hopefully, those of others as well.

I once read that weavers of Oriental carpets deliberately put one error into each rug, to illustrate that only God is perfect. Instead of making ourselves, and everybody around us, miserable trying to be perfect, can we learn to accept that there are no perfect houses, no perfect schools, no perfect jobs, no perfect churches, no perfect neighborhoods, no perfect children, no perfect adults?

Maybe that's even good news! After all, if the world were perfect, what would there be for any of us to learn or do?

Courage is not the absence of fear,
it is the mastery of it.
Anonymous

O ur third-story windows, thirty feet above ground, simply had to be washed. Since I was most bothered by them, the family voted that I should be the one to wash them.

Terrified, I climbed a forty-foot extension ladder carrying a bucket and a rag.

At the bottom the ladder shook almost uncontrollably. "I'll never make it up," I whimpered.

"Keep climbing," my husband called from the safe ground. "It gets sturdier the higher you get." Easy for him to say!

He was right. The higher you climb, the sturdier an extension ladder does get. Your own weight steadies it.

Extension ladders are a lot like life. We start out on a new venture shaky and insecure. We climb a step or two, quake, and yearn to return to our starting place and forget the whole plan.

Those who continue to put one foot above the other, however, who keep moving toward a goal, discover that the further we get, the more secure we are. Getting to the top feels magnificent!

Most of the fear that spoils our life
comes from attacking difficulties before we get to them.
Frank Crane

Tonight the winds begin to rise
And roar from yonder dropping day;
The last red leaf is whirled away,
The rooks are blown about the skies.

Alfred, Lord Tennyson

W e woke to a celestial sporting event. Buckets of hail poured on our roof while the gale winds roared approval and smacked tall trees around like they were grass.

Later we learned that tornados had touched down all over town. Thousands, including us, were without power. After a cold breakfast, we surveyed our damage. Two enormous pines had been uprooted and posed a threat to the street. Our lawn was littered with twigs and limbs. What a mess!

We had planned a peaceful family weekend: read a little, clean a little, work in the yard a bit, then drive to the mountains on Sunday afternoon. That strong wind changed our plans, rearranged our priorities, changed how we spent our time.

It also forged new friendships with neighbors as we swapped labor with chain saws and swept the street together. It brought our family closer as we struggled to stack logs, made brushwood "forts" of pine boughs, and eventually ate dinner by candlelight.

As we talked after dinner, we agreed: sometimes in life, when storms beyond our control sweep our lives, they may give us the opportunity to exchange something good for something even better.

A n architect friend was showing me his new home. "There's a different feel here," I told him, "but I don't know what it is."

He smiled. "It's the light. I looked for a house with good light in the rooms we use the most. Light lifts the spirit."

Light is also good for our bodies. Some scientists believe that people who get depressed during winter may not be getting enough sunlight. It is important to go outside on winter mornings to let our bodies absorb rays from the sun.

Modern buildings often obstruct natural light. Some are windowless, others have tinted glass to turn light away. People study, work, shop, and play in the glare of electric bulbs. There is little splendor there. Nothing to feed bodies or souls.

Since talking with our architect friend, I have begun to seek ways to use light to create peace and beauty in our home.

We now choose new homes by the amounts of physical light they get. We like to eat in dining rooms flooded with morning sun, welcome guests in living spaces that are bright and cheerful.

Where a house is dreary, we wash it in rainbows from window prisms or stained glass, set it aglow with candles and evening fires, put vases of bright flowers in dark corners. We love how rooms become magical in candlelight or moonlight.

Harder, but just as important, is to fill a home with another kind of light: order, truth, praise, encouragement, peace. Those are as necessary as physical light— maybe more so. They refresh all who live in the home and those who only pause there for a season.

When the lamps of a house are lighted
it is like the flowering of lotus on the lake.

Chinese Proverb

To accumulate possessions is to deliver pieces of oneself to dead things.

Philip Slater

othing dulls the sparkle of a home faster than clutter. Not real dirt, but piles of old newspapers, stray socks, dishes we seldom use, magazines spilling across the carpet.

Clearing out clutter can be hard. How do we know what we may need next week, next year?

One helpful criterion that can help us keep clutter down to a manageable mass was given in a newspaper interview with Chicago art dealer Ruth Volid: "I have taken care not to clutter up my space with things that have no meaning in my life."

Volid's criterion helps us ask not merely "Do we need or use this?" but "Does this have meaning in our life?" It helps us, when we move or clean closets, to decide what to put in the next garage sale. It helps us decide what magazines to subscribe to, what household appliances to buy, which sales to attend.

The same question applies to other parts of life as well. It's easy to clutter our minds with silly books and inane television shows, our time with pointless meetings and shallow relationships, our daily schedule with errands that could be combined or even left undone. When life gets cluttered it is time to ask: "Which of these have real meaning in my life?"

One ought never to buy anything except with love.
André Gide

If there were dreams to sell,
What would you buy?

Thomas Lovell Beddoes

One evening before we moved we left our sons, three and six, watching television while we said a brief farewell to neighbors. We arrived home to find the boys in a state of great excitement.

"There's a secret room in our house!" they shouted.

Proudly they displayed an enormous hole they had chiseled in the plaster, and light shining through the lath.

We were dismayed and horrified. We knew what had happened. When we had removed a picture over the couch, the nail had also fallen out. Through that pinhole the boys had seen light from the room beyond. Buoyed by hope and dreams, they had set out to explore.

Alas, that evening there was no secret room—just a whole lot of repair work we had not planned on doing. But I could understand their hope for a secret room. I sometimes dream that I live in a small, cramped house, then one day wander into a light, spacious place and discover, to my astonishment and delight, that it is also mine. Does everyone long to find, somewhere, a secret room?

Most houses do not have secret rooms, but all spirits do—they are possibilities within us that we have not yet explored. Have I, perhaps, inherited my mother's talent for painting? Could you become a dancer? Could we one day really do something significant about world suffering? See all seven continents? Become patient people, weavers of peace?

Let us not ignore our questions and dreams. They are pinpricks of light through the walls of our spirit, encouraging us to tear down walls and look for rooms we have yet to discover.

It is better to know some of the questions than all of the answers.
James Thurber

Things unseen have a light of their own.
Raoul Plus

There are souls in the world who have the gift
of finding joy everywhere,
and leaving it behind them when they go.
Their influence is an inevitable gladdening of the heart.
They give light without meaning to shine.

F. W. Faber

y grandmother must have been a light person. She raised nine children on a farm in days when keeping house meant time-consuming hard work. What her sons remember about her, however, is that Grandmother was always ready to stop what she was doing to join a child in looking at a sunset, picking wildflowers, or admiring a butterfly on the hydrangea bush.

She died before I was born, but I think of her every time I leave my sink to share a son's delight in a tit-mouse at our feeder, or leave the computer to admire a sunset with my husband. The dishes will wait. The computer is not going anywhere. But a titmouse and a sunset are fleeting joys that must be shared when they occur.

Do you think it is only a little thing to possess a house
from which lovely things can be seen?

Saint Teresa of Avila

onnie radiates light from a wheelchair. When she expressed a desire for a house of her own, some people worried. "How will you manage?" they asked. "Very well," she replied.

In her house, doorways are wide to accomodate her chair; light switches are low and enlarged, for easy reach. She discarded her stove and installed a low counter with a microwave, toaster oven, and hot plate she can reach from her chair. She had a ramp poured off her patio so she can wheel herself into her backyard and feed squirrels. A computer lets her work full-time at home.

Bonnie's home was a haven for me during a hectic time in my life. I knew that I would always find there a slower pace, a friend who would listen and never be rushing off somewhere else.

Bonnie expands my world everytime I'm with her. Not because she calls attention to problems she has with living, but because she rejoices when she overcomes the problems. Bonnie is a "light person." She shows me again and again that nothing is impossible just because it's hard.

nnah is from South Africa. She and her husband came to the United States from Soweto—the all-black southwest township of Johannesburg—so that her husband could get his Ph.D. Her home had been two rooms without electricity or running water. She had never seen a vacuum cleaner or operated a dishwasher.

She and her daughters visited us for two weeks one summer. Daily Annah rose and started to clean my house. When I urged her to be a guest instead, she shook her head. "Oh, you have such a lovely home. It is a joy to clean."

A joy to clean? For me, cleaning was something I did when company was coming, when I began to stick to the floor, or could not see out the window. Certainly something to do only if I couldn't think of anything better to do!

"I love to polish," Annah told me, making my sink gleam. "In Soweto, women polish their buckets until they shine. We are proud of what we have."

Seeing Annah's delight in cleaning—and feeling a little guilty that she was working so hard in my house—I began to work with her. I discovered how much joy there can be in mopping a floor, polishing wood until it glows, lifting clean dishes from piles of suds, folding sweet-smelling clothes.

I am grateful to Annah. She taught me to take joy in performing the tasks that bring light and sparkle to my home.

I know a little garden close,
Set thick with lily and red rose,
Where I would wander if I might
From dewy morn to dewy night,
And have one with me wandering.

William Morris

ach house has certain charms to be enjoyed. A sunny deck just right for reading. Pleasant paths for afternoon strolls. A neighborhood full of historical sites. A porch with rockers and swing.

I am saddened to realize how seldom I ever read in the sunshine, stroll in the woods, or enjoy the historical sites. The delights to which I looked forward get put aside for things I will not remember doing. Why do I let that happen?

There is more to life than increasing its speed.

Mahatma Ghandi

A house at night wears a new and different face. Unable to sleep, I prowl the dim rooms, silvered by a cantaloupe moon. Perched on the couch, I listen to noises I never hear during the day: the hum of the refrigerator, the creak of a gently moving porch swing, the rustle of a branch tenderly touching a screen. If I am very still, I can feel the house breathe.

By day the house is an inanimate shell for all we are and do. At night it hovers, broods. Like a brave and caring sentinel, it stands guard over vulnerable sleepers and provides a haven for the restless.

Usually at night I refresh myself by sleep. But once in a while I like to rise in the middle of the night, creep down the stairs, sit in the dark, and commune with the spirit of my house.

. . . Nature is never spent;
There lives the dearest freshness deep down things.
Gerard Manley Hopkins

The problem is usually not the problem,
but what you do with the problem.

Bruce Sladek

fter friends moved into their new home, they discovered it had been built over springs. For over a year they argued with the builder, trying to get him to properly cap the springs and drain the lawn. They were frustrated and frequently out of temper. Finally they decided that the problem was taking a greater toll on their family than it was worth. "We decided to forgive the builder and get on with living," they announced. They hired someone else who capped springs. They dug drainage ditches and resodded the lawn. By the next year, instead of living with bitterness, they were hosting parties in their basement den and playing volleyball on the grass.

When something goes wrong—in our houses or in our lives—we can get caught up in blame and bitterness. But there is an option: forgive those who wrong us and do what we can to remedy the situation. That keeps problems from becoming *real* problems.

We must make our homes
centers of compassion and forgive endlessly.

Mother Theresa

I like to have clean windows—especially when it's lovely outside. But a problem with clean windows is that they do show me the world beyond my own home.

The world out there is such a mess! Two-thirds of the people don't have enough to eat. Hundreds of thousands are homeless. Millions of children need food, medicine and education. There's a lonely woman just down my street.

It's easier to think of my home as four walls to shelter me from life's storms than as a window opening onto the rest of the world. And it is so easy for me to get absorbed in my home and ignore the world outside and

those who live about me. I think, "I really should call
Jane," then I notice that the coffee table needs dusting. I
dream, "Someday I'll stop talking about the hunger
problem and really do something about it," but it is
easier to stay in my house and enjoy what I like best—
reading, soft music, snacks to nibble, a sewing machine.

That's when I need to wash windows, to remind me
that my home is only one room in the house that is the
world.

Thank you, Lord, for my eyes,
windows open on the wide world.
Michel Quoist

Now first, as I shut the door,
I was alone
In the new house . . . .

Edward Thomas

I am not a pioneer at heart. I enjoy reading stories about adventurous people who cross stormy seas and establish new homes on foreign soil. Genesis is one of my favorite books. But the truth is, I would never voluntarily have left an eighteenth century London drawing room for a log cabin in Virginia, or a snug Scottish croft for a sod house in Colorado. My soul yearns to take root deep in one acre of ground, to watch small trees grow tall as my hair grows gray.

Yet that is not the life to which I have been called. In this world, many of us will move, and move, and move yet again.

"After a while all the people begin to look the same," a Navy wife once told me. I know what she means. In a new place, I spend several weeks noticing who this person looks like, what problems that person has in common with someone I knew elsewhere. I am overwhelmed by deciding who to reach out to, what to become involved in.

One day early in a new city I was feeling especially sorry for myself. My friends were scattered around the globe, my heart didn't feel like it could reach out to people again knowing that new ties could be severed with yet another move. "I have nothing left to give," I cried. "I am given out!"

Suddenly my son ran to me and announced: "Our play dough has died." Sadly he held out the tin to show me a wad of dried-up pink concrete, unworked and exposed to air for weeks.

"You didn't use it," I told him. "Dough needs to be kneaded."

"Like people?" he asked. "You said they need to be needed, too!"

I knew we weren't using the same words, but he was right. People do need to be needed—and kneaded, living to the fullest wherever we are.

May life open up to you, door by door;
May you find in yourself the ability to trust it,
And the courage to give to the most difficult
the most confidence of all.
Ranier Maria Rilke

Almighty God,
keep this home in your continual care.
Put far from it, we pray, every root of bitterness
and false pride. Fill it with faith, virtue, knowledge,
temperance, patience, and godliness.
Knit together those who come under its roof,
and send them forth from this place to love
and serve you.

Adapted from The Book of Common Prayer

T he electrician shook his head in disbelief. "You haven't blown out a single appliance? Lady, the way those wires were connected, you should have blown every major appliance you have, maybe even burned down."

I had called him because of a minor nuisance: flickering lights. He found a major problem: someone had forgotten to fully connect all wires to the box when we had built the house three years before. As he completed his work and left, he said, "Lady, you are an incredibly lucky woman."

When he had gone, I said a prayer of thanksgiving. I knew, you see, that I wasn't "incredibly lucky." I had been protected.

I remembered an evening when special friends had trooped across the subflooring between studs of our walls-to-be, trying to imagine what the finished house would look like.

"After all those old houses, can you believe you'll finally live in a new one?" someone joked.

"A finished kitchen!" chimed in another. "Can you stand it?"

Suddenly one woman stood still and reached for our hands. "I want to dedicate this house right now, even before it's completed."

Together we knelt on plywood subflooring to pray that this would be God's house, used for God's purposes and to God's glory. And we prayed that God would keep it safe.

It took three years for me to learn just how safe God had kept it—and us within it!

❖

Cover design, page layout,
type and production to camera-ready
by Markus Frey, Stamford, CT.

May the Lord watch over this house.
May the Lord keep those who dwell here from all harm.
May the Lord watch over your life
and over your coming and going,
both now and forever more.

Adapted from Psalm 121

❖